LACE AT THE WINDOWS OF HEAVEN

A fresh look at bobbin lace

by Jean Mary Eke

In memory of my parents, George and Elsie Tudor, who made this book possible.

Jean Mary Eke 2007©
photographs by Alexandra Stillwell 2007
First published in the UK 2007 by
Salex Publishing
26 Willow Park, Haywards Heath, West Sussex, RH16 3UA, UK
e-mail: alexstillwell@talktalk.net

Reproduction of the 'Genesis Initial' from the Winchester Bible,
by permission of the Chapter of Winchester Cathedral.

Reproduction of the 'The Chichester Roundel' a wall painting in the Bishop's Chapel,
by permission of the Bishop of Chichester, The Right Reverend John Hind.

Reproduction of 'The Dog and Rabbit' from the Macclesfield Psalter,
by permission of the Fitzwilliam Museum, Cambridge.

All rights reserved
No part of this book may be reproduced or
transmitted in any form or by any means, electronic or
mechanical, including photocopying, recording or any
information storage or retrieval system,
without prior permission in writing from the author.

One, two buckle my shoe.
Three, four knock at the door.
Five, six pick up sticks.
Seven, eight lay them straight.
Nine, ten a big, fat hen.

Lace tell, anon.

ISBN 978-0-9554694-8-0

Printed and bound in Great Britain by Ditchling Press Ltd.

ONE, TWO BUCKLE MY SHOE

There are so many clichés about life being 'woven' or 'like a tapestry' that I hesitate to add 'lacemaking' to the list. Yet lace, to me, qualifies best of all. Lace can best be described as a fabric of holes joined together by threads. This very structure is designed to allow light to pass through and, as in life, it is often easier to see the holes and, only in hindsight, to be conscious of the connecting threads. Somehow, in my search to make lace in a way which satisfies me, I have found subjects and a way which has let the light through in many ways, and this is what I want to share with you my fellow lacemakers and friends.

Let me begin by telling you something about myself. I was born in the Lancashire cotton town of Burnley, whilst the weaving sheds were still in operation, so perhaps weaving is in my genes. In 1950 my family moved to Norwich. The sunshine and blue East Anglian skies were exciting after the grey days of Burnley. We had very little extra money, but each Saturday my mother took my younger brother and me exploring in Norwich which is richly endowed with history and art. Much of the city's early wealth had come from the woollen industry, and the Bridewell Museum had looms and shawls woven in Norwich with the Indian patterns we know as Paisley. Weaving was my first love and I was lucky to go to a school where 'craft' was taught as a subject alongside 'art'. I was to train to be a teacher and was encouraged to widen my knowledge and increase my range of subjects which included ancient history and New Testament studies. I received the Mrs Coppings Prize for Craft in the form of a King James Edition Bible. I was a Sunday school teacher and, looking back, I cannot remember a time when church life and God's love were not present. I had been born on a Sunday morning, and as a small child, I had been pleased that my parents had got that right, at least.

Scarf in wool & lurex

Using a table loom borrowed from school, my mother and I explored its possibilities. We used wool and the sparkly gold and silver lurex threads just becoming available. I remember making a set of bonnet, mittens and scarf in bottle green wool, narrow velvet ribbon and lurex threads and wearing them for my interview at Whitelands College, Putney. I was accepted to train as a secondary school teacher specialising in weaving and pottery. Whitelands and her May Queens had been beloved by John Ruskin, and there was a strong link with the Arts and Crafts Movement. I was young and not nearly as aware as I should have been. However, an outing of the college Art and Craft department to Sussex, to visit the community of families of artist craftsmen at Ditchling Common, had a profound effect on me. It was Catholic Christian Socialism in an artistic environment, and I was intrigued. Now in 2007, living in Sussex, I drive through Ditchling at least once a week, and this booklet is printed by Ditchling Press, almost the last remnant of that community. Today much of my inspiration comes from the sources used by these craftsmen.

After college my life changed radically when I married and then lived in the West Indies for nine years. At a secondary school on the small island of Nevis I taught every subject except craft, but I did have a large loom on which to experiment. Alas it was too big for me and life was too full. On our return in 1971 to the UK, interest in crafts was growing. My mother had taken up bobbin lace and encouraged me to have a try. We lived at opposite ends of the country so it was not often that we could work together. Using the Womens' Institute to find a class at Basingstoke Technical college I started making lace. The class was run by Mrs Bright of Hampshire W.I and I took the W.I certificates in Lacemaking, following that with the W.I Demonstrator and Teachers' Certificates in 1976. An elderly lady, living directly opposite me, had illustrated her mother's book on lacemaking. She was Winifred Brooke, the daughter of Margaret Brooke, author of 'Lace in the Making with Bobbins and Needle' 1923. Books on lace were few and far between, in those days, and I avidly read her book and anything else I could find. I used 'Bobbin Lace Work' by Margaret Maidment 1931, and read 'The Art of Bobbin Lace' by Louis Tebbs 1907. They all gave me insights into lacemaking and designing of individual patterns and I desperately wanted to create my own style.

THREE, FOUR KNOCK AT THE DOOR

What is lace?

It certainly comes to us with a great deal of imagery. It is associated with the high points of life; births, christenings, weddings and functions, in or out of church or fashion. It can look grubby, tatty, kitsch and be associated with Miss Haversham and even arsenic. But great expectations are always there; it can look magnificent.

How do we define such a textile? Let me repeat, lace is a fabric of holes connected together, and as such allows light to pass through. What is present on both sides of the fabric is important to its effect. Few of us fail to recognise the beauty of bare or snow clad trees in winter, against a bright blue or sunset orange sky; seeing the colour through the tracery of branches brings the colour forward to us and we respond.

Lace, as a fabric, can be made by way of many techniques. It can be made using a single thread as in knitting and crochet, or with many as in my own bobbin lace. Bobbin lace developed from plaiting and weaving. For the pattern we use a drawing, geometrical or freestyle, drawn on card. This is pinned onto a pillow, traditionally stuffed with straw firmly enough to support pins. Pins are placed in holes, already pricked in the pattern, and these support the threads in position. The threads are wound onto bobbins, and you proceed as in weaving; the workers are the weft and the passives the warp. We can trace the origins and development of lace by the study of portraits and monuments; the beginning roughly corresponding with the time that pins became freely available in the mid 16th century. It is of interest to note that all designs for embroidery, frescos, tapestries etc. were transferred from one medium to another by pouncing; that is by banging a small bag of charcoal dust along a line of small holes pricked along the line of the drawing. These dust points could then be joined up on the new cloth or parchment. A ready-made lace pattern perhaps? As you look closely at early lace you often see little birds and cherubs peeping out, and sometimes more elaborate pictorial scenes.

Lacemaking styles and techniques passed quickly along the trade routes of Europe, and were soon made in very many places. Over time local styles and techniques were developed, and we now recognise lace by generic terms such as Bedfordshire, Brussels, Bucks Point, Honiton and Milanese.

To a non-lacemaker a working pillow, the 'big-fat-hen' of the nursery rhyme, piled high with bunches and bundles of bobbins, seems to present an impossible task, but it is comforting to know that you work with only four bobbins at any one moment. Also, by working directly on the pattern, you can always find your starting position. I feel that this may be a reason for its popularity in convents, when the day was constantly being broken up by the call of the bell to the daily offices. The Sisters would have had a working knowledge of the illustrations in Bibles and Psalters, and might even have used the actual discarded artists' drafts.

A big fat hen

In earlier times, the lace any one person could produce would depend on where they lived and who their teacher was. The patterns were jealously guarded, and often a lacemaker only had access to part of a design. In the last 25 years many more books have been published on the history of lace and manuals containing the techniques used for making lace. The knowledge is now there for all to find.

1977 was a very good year. It was the Queen's Silver Jubilee, I passed my driving licence my West Indian one having lapsed, and I started to wear contact lenses. The difference in my eyesight was a revelation; I no longer saw the world in soft focus, even the grass had sharp edges. It was like living

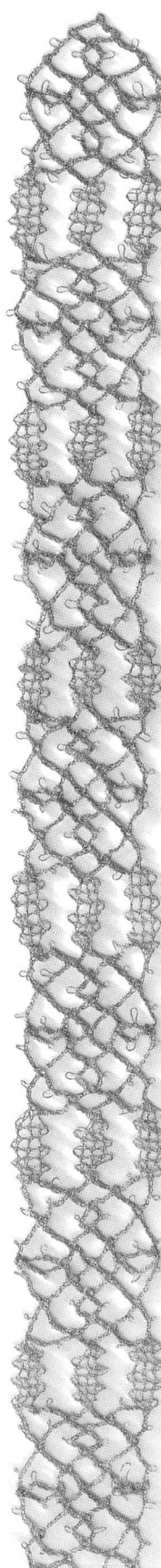

From Le Pompe 1559, Pattern 15D, Book 2

in a Rousseau painting. Needless to say, my lace improved. I had not heard of lacemaking as a current craft when I studied weaving at college but, looking back, the seeds were already there. I had used the light-catching metallic threads and one of my exam pieces was an open weave curtain. It was of natural linen with gossamer grey and yellow wool to let in the light. I was fascinated to see that metallic threads had been used in Tudor times for plaited lace; the famous Holbein portrait of Henry VIII shows Henry wearing a gold lace collar over a soft, white neckband. That same year, I went to the Victoria & Albert Museum and had 'Le Pompe', 1560, lace pattern book copied, and set about trying to recreate the lace using the new threads available. I found that these threads were not sufficiently pliable and, as Santina Levey says in her 'History of Lace', "The patterns are not easy to work and many of the intersections are extremely complicated". I tried to use this source to design gold work for church vestments. The ideas were good, my techniques limited and I was working on my own. In the end I felt that the results did not justify the time spent. Embroidery would serve the purpose better.

In those days textile design was changing, embroidery was becoming exciting and I wanted to do the same for lace. I was fairly proficient at drafting Torchon patterns and was successful in using D.M.C. metallic threads. I found they worked well as long as you cut down the number of twists you would normally use. I made a set of Alice bands for a bride and her bridesmaids and gold doyleys for the posies for an Easter Sunday wedding. I used mohair and lurex to edge a shawl and continued to experiment with wire and string in the true post 1960s style. But when I tried to improvise with these elements the results, to put it mildly, were dissatisfying. What looked good on paper, and even in the making on the pillow, had the unfortunate tendency to distort when removed from the supporting pins. There was little long-term use for such items, I began to lose heart. My interest in lace remained, I continued to visit museums, looking at all types of lace and continued buying lace books and reading all that was available.

My husband, Robert, was 20 years my senior so I planned to restart making lace when we 'retired'. Alas, as soon as that happened, Robert had a devastating stroke and I became Carer 1st Class from then onwards. After seven years I realised that I would have to make a big effort if I were to accomplish anything. I managed to get a respite weekend with Ann Collier at West Dean. I had just missed meeting her all those years before. There I met Anne and Tina Talbot, sisters-in-law, who befriended a very tired and lost me, and they introduced me to Southwick Lace Class and Rosemary Brown who had just taken over the class. We all became friends and, with Rosemary, I attended another lace weekend at West Dean this time to be taught by Alexandra Stillwell.

Alex had started lace about the same time as myself. She also has a teaching background, but had the advantage of coming from maths and science. She had been based in Essex and was in touch with the lacemakers of Buckinghamshire and Bedfordshire and had been a prominent member of the Lace Guild. She has all the knowledge and skills that I needed. We soon became friends; she took me under her wing and has been the most generous teacher anyone could wish for. Still a carer, I was encouraged to take breaks and I used these to attend lace weekends. I was lucky to be able to attend courses by Sandra Langworthy, Sandi Woods, Pat Read and Pat Perryman. I was befriended by many other lacemakers in this way. You may, by now, think that I am one of those people who sits in class and to whom everything comes easily, first go. Think again, I invariably struggle at first; it usually takes some time before the stitch, or pattern, 'clicks in'. Margaret Maidment tells you to watch your lace, not your hands. I never imagined I would reach the exalted state when such a thing would happen. With Alex's help and encouragement I revised my earlier designing skills and began to think of my future direction.

I had no daughter to make wedding gifts for and had no need for table linen, but I continued to be fascinated by old lace and the words, in 1926, of Margaret Brooke. Her introduction 'Let the expert sweep aside the cramping fetters of tradition and use this loom (bobbins, pillow and pins) to work out the fancies of a fertile brain, and mankind will have a lace of novel, as well as beautiful texture, to admire. Woman as an inventor is no longer remarkable!' What I lacked in daughters I made up for in friends. Over the years we had kept in touch with people all over the country and, indeed, the world. Our Christmas card mailing list was huge. I would design patterns, which we could photograph and then print. I would keep the lace but be able to share the sentiment. Life was not easy in the isolation of my life as a 'carer', but this would keep the joy of Christmas and Christmases past, ever present.

FIVE, SIX PICK UP STICKS
The Three Ships

By now my lacemaking skills had progressed. I had a greater understanding of the spread of threads across the work and how relative densities and twistings controlled the dynamics of the end product. I was ready for my second 'take off'. Where would I begin? I had learnt to make a Milanese scroll and saw its possibilities. What about the 'Three Ships'? I built up a pile of pictures, drawings and photographs of the sea, Japanese prints being a most fruitful source. I could certainly use the scroll for a white horse.

Saint Jerome from 'Paleographia Sacra Pictoria', 1843,

Then I looked for ships, and they were everywhere from galleons to dinghies. Then in 'Paleographia Sacra Pictoria', 1843, a little ship seemed to be sailing straight for me. This illumination, originally from a 9th century French bible, shows Saint Jerome setting off from Rome to sail to Bethlehem. Here he was to translate the Bible from Hebrew and Greek into Latin, the universal language, thereby making the texts available to all. East meets West. As I looked, I saw that the prow could be another scroll, and the modest quantity of rigging and a single sail would be manageable. I traced and redrew, dividing the boat into sections workable in lace. Alex had taught me to look at the smallest and largest sections.

Experience had taught me that if a clothwork (woven) area was too large the workers would not be able to control the passives and the tension would be lost. If the spaces were too small they would not work as design elements and there would be insufficient room for sewings. By looking at each individual section, and judging its place in the whole, I was able to choose an appropriate method for working each part. I had the skills and resources and began to work in silk thread. I have found silk an ideal thread for this type of work. Floss, a very lightly twisted continuous silk thread, will spread and form good clothwork. Spun silk can give a rather flat effect, but nothing beats the continuous yarn, which reflects light with a glow of its own and brings a picture to life. The threads can be packed densely or allowed to spread as required.

I considered working the whole sea in lace, and argued with myself as to whether it was valid. If I used too fine a thread the work would not keep its shape alongside the main motifs, yet, if a thicker thread was used this would prove too dominant. Again, looking at lace as an embellishment to brocades and appliquéd onto machine net or voile, I felt I would be justified in appliquéing my waves and ships onto blue slub silk. This allowed the blue to show through, and therefore to be an integral part of the design, introducing an element of colour and thereby suggesting a sunny sea and sky.

Prepared sketch of the ship

I began to work. and in due time, removed my first ship from my pillow. It held together, and I realised I was 'in business'. My techniques needed smartening up. The edges needed more careful definition, and I gave it a 'could do better' mark. But Alex was there and, with her wider experience, saw my lace in context and encouraged me. She suggested that, for the two ships further away, I scaled the pattern down and used progressively finer threads to increase the feeling of depth and space. I completed the smaller ships and returned to repeat the main ship. I had fun finding a Brussels flower and then a crown in an ancient piece of lace, and used them to decorate the sail with the rose and crown of Our Lady Queen of Heaven. (Yes, a pub sign.) I found a dove that could pass as seagull, maybe. There is even a leviathan (Lock Ness monster) if you look hard enough. Taking a break whilst working the main ship on Good Friday, I looked up 'ship' in my book of symbols. As expected it was given as a symbol of the Christian Church which, like Noah's Ark, carries the faithful safely over the perilous seas of life. It concluded with 'The ship is usually depicted with a mast in the form of a cross, symbolising redemption through the Cross of Christ. This was something the original artist knew all about and I had instinctively placed them as on Calvary. Some ideas were there from the beginning, others came as I worked. It was lace I was weaving, not embroidery, and I was satisfied – for the time being.

'I saw Three Ships' completed Christmas 2003

SEVEN, EIGHT LAY THEM STRAIGHT
The Chichester Roundel

The Chichester Roundel c.1220

For me, working on one piece sets me off on planning the next and I soon found myself faced with a mountain to climb. I had begun to realise that a wall painting in the chapel of the Bishop's Palace, Chichester, known as the Chichester Roundel, is very special indeed. It is a picture of Our Lady and the Christchild enthroned within a quatrefoil frame. The Christchild is standing on His mother's knee, facing her and pulling her head towards His, a very recognisable gesture of love. This Roundel has been dated to 1220-1240a.d. by comparing the style with English embroideries (Opus Anglicanum.) I felt here was a design I could make in lace. Light is present; the quatrefoil frame acts as a window between heaven and earth. Our Lady's robes spread out in front of the inner frame and she appears to be bringing Heaven to Earth. The light is coming from Our Lady to the viewer. Dare I use such a drawing? The original artist would in all probability have drawn for embroiderers, so, with the Bishop's permission I began to plan my own interpretation.

There were two main challenges. First, the frame had to be perfectly executed as a static foil to the central design. The outer circle is in three rows, Father, Son and Holy Spirit, whilst the inner quatrefoil has two rows representing Father and Holy Spirit, whilst the Son is the focus of the central space. Thus the frame would have to be carefully worked; there would be no room for 'mistakes' to be interpreted as 'texture' or 'proof of hand-made'. Many samples of suitable braids were worked, but, in the end, I opted for the simplest; just bands of cloth and half stitch. I made sure that the proportions of the rows would balance and that the whole would keep its shape on completion. The pattern was pricked with geometric accuracy. The addition of a Widhof roll along the edges, with extra threads along the outer edge, gave greater definition, and a spun silk thread gave a matt finish. For the frame I used a large, flattish pillow and then moved to a large, more raised pillow for the second, and greater challenge, the figures in the central space.

By now the picture was imprinting itself on my brain and as with The Three Ships various sections chose their own lace stitches. The Bucks Point lattice filling was very obvious for the back of the throne and Bucks Point ground would make a nice contrast for the dresses. One of the characteristics of Opus Anglicanum embroidery was the portrayal of flowing garments, with the use of split stitching and underside couching to convey shading and movement. I would have to find a way of doing this in lace. The outer robes of Our Lady had lost most of their defining lines but I sketched these in, dividing the areas into workable sections. My freestyle patterns are not pre-pricked. I work directly onto a photocopy of my prepared drawing. Choosing my stitches carefully I used half stitch for the shadows; the larger spaces between the threads allowing the darker background of the mount to show through. The denser areas of cloth stitch reflect and therefore suggest light.

People often ask 'How do you know where to begin?' The real question is 'Where do you finish?' All those threads have to be sewn in and sewn away to produce a fabric that will hold together and look neat on both sides. The optimum start is often one that you would rather leave until you have had some practice. In this case, I began with Our Lady's crown and had to tackle her face early on. I persuaded myself, that if I had to make a second attempt, I should not have wasted much time. Did you know that the nursery rhyme 'One, two buckle my shoe' refers to a young lacemaker preparing to go to school and getting ready to work the stitch we know as 'ten stick' or 'rib'. The funny thing is that this stitch can be worked with 8-14 bobbins (sticks). I use this rib to 'draw' the lines and the number of bobbins I use depends on how dominant the line needs to be. Thinking back to my weaving, when I filled in these lines with cloth stitch, I was weaving small areas of 'tabby cloth'.

The Roundel photographed at the window against the multicoloured background of the garden, completed Spring 2006

Prepared drawing of The Roundel

The finished Roundel inverted

*This scene in the Macclesfield Psalter, points to Psalm 8.
'O Lord our Governor, how excellent is thy Name in all the world:
thou hast set thy glory above the heavens!'
The first psalm for Sunday Mattins*

Rabbit and Dog at the organ in Heaven, completed Spring 2007.

The Rabbit and Dog

I fell in love with the little rabbit the first time I saw him making music on the front cover of the Church Times, advertising the exhibition The Cambridge Illuminations at The Fitzwilliam Museum, in 2005, which included the special exhibition of the Art Fund's newly purchased Macclesfield Psalter. I travelled to Cambridge and found that the Rabbit playing the organ is the final scene of an epic tale told in the margins of the psalter. The tiny picture is barely 5cm long. Previous scenes tell the story of a world where unexpected things happen and roles are reversed.

First a rabbit goes hunting, riding on the back of a dog. The rabbit is enthusiastically blowing a horn. The next scene shows the same rabbit and dog jousting. Jousts were not meant to be deadly combats but the dog, showing a degree of doggy glee, mortally skewers the surprised rabbit with his lance. The rabbit family mourns, and then there is the funeral. Two rabbits carry the bier on their shoulders following a black rabbit who tolls a bell in either paw, glancing over his shoulder to make sure all is progressing well. The rear is taken by a priest rabbit, in vestments, sprinkling holy water. The vestments and the coffin pall are not black, as you would expect, but are red and gold striped. These are Holy Relics. Finally the rabbit is shown in heaven, once more ' calling the tune'. This time he is playing a tiny pipe organ. The surprise is that the dog is there too, with his ears and tail down he is looking penitent, never the less as the worker of the bellows he is summoning the wind of The Holy Spirit and being the enabler of the Heavenly Harmony. The rabbit has completely forgiven him.

Later as I worked the piece of lace I found that my feelings shifted towards this little dog and even more so when Brillo, a Patterdale terrier, came to visit. He had all the little expressions of the medieval dog. This final drawing shows the two animals making music on an extended leafy branch. I took this drawing and framed it with other marginal drawings from the psalter; perfect for them to sit in its shade. The oak sapling was obvious and I included ivy leaves and the artists spray of flowers. It is fascinating how all these motifs occur throughout history in embroidery, carving and indeed lace itself. I could choose my stitches from many sources. The addition of picots and a rolled edging on the Brussels flower suggested the sepals of the original drawing; I could use the scroll again at the base of the tree trunk. In all, it gave me scope to use many more skills. Mrs Brooke had warned against using too many fillings and stitches in one work, but somehow the exuberance of the subject allowed me to play with the animals. I particularly enjoyed working the organ. The original drawing was so tiny that there was little detail, but I could suggest wood with a Russian braid , and carving with Bedfordshire raised work. My organ pipes could have openings and decoration with Milanese archway and four-pin spot. In many ways, the tiny ivy leaf was the biggest challenge, but I found that scrolling round the inner angles and back stitching at the points worked.

I love to quote from the artist Lucien Freud, 'A moment of complete happiness never occurs in the creation of a work of art. The promise of it is felt in the act of creation, but it disappears toward the completion of the work. For it is then that the painter realises that it is only a picture he is painting, until then he had almost dared to hope that the picture might spring to life'. This was very true of me and the Rabbit and Dog.

The Nativity of Christ from the Winchester Bible

The Nativity from the Genesis Initial of The Winchester Bible c.1160 to c.1175.

As I write this in preparation for printing, I am working on the lace for the front cover, a Nativity. Each piece I work draws me into the next, and there is even a sense in which the pictures seem to choose me. This time I am using the Genesis Initial of The Winchester Bible c.1160 to c.1175 which uses Saint Jerome's translation. At first I was looking for a companion piece for The Roundel, but a large angel on either side did not inspire me. Then I remembered the wall paintings at St Mary's, West Chiltington. Here the scenes of the life of Our Lady, are framed in an arcade of quatrefoil arches. Again these are stylistically connected to Early English embroidery in the Victoria and Albert Museum, the very copes I had so often left Robert snoozing amongst whilst I went to study lace. They also connect with The Chichester Roundel. The scenes themselves at Chiltington are only just discernable. Perhaps I could start with the first, The Annunciation, and only one angel, Gabriel. Then looking at the unusual angles of the very faint Nativity scene, I realised that it echoed the Nativity medallion of the Winchester Bible Genesis Initial. Before Robert's retirement we had worked in Winchester Diocese, and I checked my sources. The design is not in the Renaissance style of Nativities with which we are so familiar. This is a very Early English style. Mary is still in bed after childbirth, she is resting her head in her hand and leaning on her elbow. She faces out of the scene, very much 'pondering these things'. Joseph, in his woolly cap, looks elderly and worried, and yet their hands are touching. The Christchild, in the manger, is centre stage to the back. An infant, He shows all the vulnerability of a baby and the swaddling bands foretell the chains of His Passion. The straw takes the place of a cushion on the crib, the royal throne. When I wondered how to portray this straw I chose to mix all my different thicknesses of silk threads randomly in half stitch. The whole human condition is present, shared and understood. What mankind does not recognise the natural order does, He is watched over by an ecstatic Ox and Ass, Isaiah chapter 1, verse 3, 'The ox knoweth his owner and the ass his master's crib'. An icon of the same period, from Saint Catherine's monastery in Sinai shows the animals licking the infant Christ with bright red tongues. They alone are recognising their Master.

The Winchester Bible is the biggest surviving 12th century Bible made in England. It is 583 cm. by 396 cm. Its sheer size would be very impressive, as it would have to be carried by two monks in procession. The Genesis Initial or the 'I' from 'In The Beginning' goes down the full length of the page and sets the scene magnificently for the rest of the Book. It shows, in seven illuminated medallions, the story of man's redemption through the Old Testament types to the New; the creation of Eve, the Flood (Noah's Ark), the sacrifice of Isaac, Moses given the tablets of the Law, the anointing of David, Christ's Nativity, the Last Judgement and the resurrection of souls.

My fingers itched to begin, not forgetting to reverse the design this type of lace is made from the back. The twelfth century bed is a delightful part of the scene and I began by outlining the folds of the sheet with a six-pair rib. Developing my own recognisable style has always been my ambition and as the work progressed I dared to

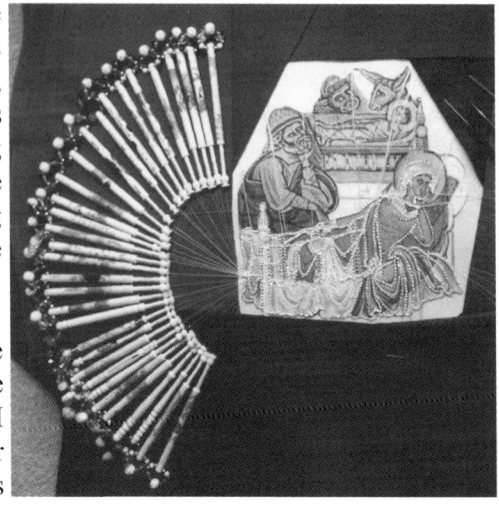

The Nativity in the making

hope that this was happening. The darker shadows were again filled in with half stitch. Later, for Saint Joseph's cloak, I used a much older technique which gave a more masculine solidity. This (Patricia Read's basketweave braid) was used in early Milanese lace for texture before half stitch was developed. It took me a whole weekend to fill in his cloak. Alas, Saint Joseph, had never had as much attention from me before and it was not long before I was realising his own importance in the scheme of things. When people hear how long it takes to make such pictures they usually shudder and dismiss the whole idea of doing likewise. But I find that the time spent on these designs has opened up interests in all manner of things. Books, already on my shelves, have been reopened. At Chichester Cathedral I have listened with new ears to early English music. Re-reading Oxford World's Classic the 'Paston Letters' I note with pleasure a reference, in a letter of 1459, to someone as a 'cunning and crafty man'. The footnote tells me the words cunning and crafty meant learned and skilful and did not yet bear a derogatory sense. This 'crafty' lady is enjoying herself.

The Nativity, completed Autumn 2007, detail.

 # NINE, TEN A BIG FAT HEN

A few more-'holesome thoughts and technical bits.

As I re-read what I have already written I am so aware of what has been left out so I continue now with just a few words for those of you who are still interested or would like to learn more. Finding a good teacher is a great help but make sure you train yourself to follow books, there are a great many to chose from these days. Lace is not a 'quick fix' craft you do not learn it at a day workshop. It is a craft that has to be worked on between classes, a bit like learning to type. Even if you cannot find a weekly class there are excellent weekend courses that you can attend, lacemakers are a friendly bunch of people.

Just as you need to know the vocabulary before you can tell a story the same goes for lace making and designing. It is the chicken and egg problem all over again. But believe me it will save a lot of frustration and heartache if you put learning the skills first, with understanding and then designing your own patterns a close second. Spend time looking closely at what other lacemakers have accomplished, both at the present time and in the past.

A long time ago I saw antique church lace with religious themes and wanted to do the same; but however hard I tried, it was just not possible until I had mastered a fair number of skills. Like Picasso, you have to first learn how to draw before you can portray pure emotion with just a few well chosen strokes of paint. I write this not to discourage designers but to encourage the process of learning the craft of lacemaking and coming to designing through a good knowledge of how the craft works.

There is no book written with all there is to know about lace and lacemaking. Alexandra Stillwell's book is *All about making*-Geometrical Bucks Point Lace and she uses 260 pages and over 600 diagrams and photographs, to show you how to make one section of one type of lace. But it could be a good place to begin.

If you have stayed with me up till now you will have realised that the subject of the pattern matters a great deal to me. You are going to spend a lot of precious time on the piece so chose a subject to which you can relate. You could develop the idea of a holiday, real or imagined; ships flowers and animals all echo down lacemaking corridors. Dragons and mystical beasts are always lurking there somewhere, look at any piece of lace you can find, old or new. See how other lace workers have tackled the subject. Find a picture to adapt or draw your own, cut and paste. Once you have found your picture have a good hard look. Does the design divide up into manageable sections, nowhere, like Alice, too large or too small? How many pairs of bobbins can you comfortably manage in a row of whole stitch? How fine will your thread need to be? Only experience will tell you. Then there are the sections, which tell you straight away what technique to use, for example the scroll for the waves in The Three Ships, the Brussels rose for the for the emblem on the ships sail, the pimpernel of the Rabbit and Dog, and the decoration on the bed drapes of the Nativity, not forgetting the Honiton picot edge for the Rabbit's tail! Do not get carried away at this stage by choosing too many interesting fillings and techniques, they will only worry the viewer and detract from the main design. Every piece does not have to be a sampler.

Size matters---- and it is best to begin with a modestly sized piece. You do not want something, which takes so long to make that you lose interest. Finish a piece, learn and move on. You may get some surprises!

Tools and Equipment

Choose the pillow and bobbins with which you are most comfortable. Most of us are familiar with a slightly domed mushroom pillow and spangled bobbins and I use mainly these myself, finding a pattern which fits easily within an A4 paper will work on a 24 ins. diameter pillow. Bobbins hanging over the edge of too small a pillow are awkward to manage and too large a pillow for your arms makes your backache. Remember if you must do something big it can always be worked in sections and joined later. Lace prickings, as we call the patterns, were before the end of the 19th century pieces of vellum with tiny holes along the design lines (hence the similarity to embroidery pouncing). When vellum became unavailable thick paper, which has rarely survived, and a thicker brown card, which we still use, took its place. The heavy card works well for geometric designs, which can be transferred accurately, and permanently to the card before work begins. The card also has the advantage of being able to be used more than once; however I do not find it as flexible as softer papers. I find that it is best not to pre-prick the pattern. I need the complete line of my drawing, and carefully place each pinhole along it as I progress. This method was the one Louisa Tebbs swore by in her book The Art Of Bobbin Lace in 1907, it keeps the eyes of the worker on the work and prevents many glitches and irregularities. Covering a drawing with sticky backed plastic does have some faults, but it ensures that the work is kept free of any marks from ink however 'permanent', and pencil marks, however well erased.

It seems obvious but best quality pins are paramount, I now use the new stainless steel pins, which, unlike the new brass ones, do not seem to mark the thread. And talking of marking the thread I was once horrified to find that some dark wooden bobbins had discoloured my silk thread. It is always a good idea to keep bobbins well wound but when you are using expensive threads and working a large piece of lace you cannot always do this. To keep every thing clean and tidy I cover work completed with a white handkerchief and have a pile of cover cloths at the ready. These are in constant use as the working lines of the bobbins are often changing. Lacemakers should know about horizon lines of a pattern and the horizon line of the drawing has also to be borne in mind. When a group of bobbins is temporally out of use it is a good idea to thread the spangles on to a large knitting pin.

You may be surprised to see that I have preferred to make this series of lace work without using coloured threads. It comes back to my thoughts on light again. After all, white is a mixture of all colours in light and the best colours are those of the imagination. In my experience, to get a density of colour in textiles you need to have a very close weave, as in tapestry or satin stitch embroidery, and somehow lace with its holes dilutes the colour too much. You can of course pack the threads in but this can give such a tight hard feel to the end product that it ceases to feel like a piece of lace. Once you have chosen the colour of a particular piece of work it fixes it in place forever. It limits the viewer to one take of the picture. Lace stitches and fillings are the 'colours' in lace. Fillings are its textures, and any textured threads will affect the final result. If in doubt, make a sample. The colour of the backgrounds finds its way through the lace. The Roundel looks well against any richly coloured background, whether it is mounted directly onto a background or placed in a double-sided Perspex frame. It was a surprise to us all how well it looked when photographed with the garden behind. The inverted 'negative' was also be striking.

This spring 2007, Alex and I visited The Bowes Museum, Barnard Castle to see the exhibition Fine and Fashionable, Lace from the Blackborne Collection. One of the six Lace Treasures which introduced the viewer to lace and to the exhibition was a strip 24 cm wide and 404 cm long. It was designed to border the length of a window drape and was displayed in a ceiling to floor case edging a curtain of translucent linen. The drape was lit from behind reminiscent of the light which would, in all probability, have shone through from the sky and Lagoon of Venice, where it was made c. 1600. The light showed the design and workmanship to perfection and the rhythms of the repeat design came alive. Lace at windows, there was my title, 'Lace At The Windows Of Heaven'.

It has been a very enjoyable process of learning on all levels as I have worked these four bobbin lace pieces. With the original artists I have thought about all manner of things, sometimes the fun of the journey ,and sometimes the struggles and deeper things of life. I have enjoyed finding the stitches for each part of a design but, above all , just sitting quietly and working the lace.

HOLES WITHOUT END, AMEN

MY THANKS TO

Alex and all those who have helped and
encouraged me and kept me on the straight
and narrow path.

BIBLIOGRAPHY

The Golden Legend, Jacobus de Voragine, translate and published by William Caxton 1483
Palaeopraphia Sacra Pictoria, 1843.
The Art of Bobbin Lace, Louisa A. Tebbs, Chapman & Hall Ltd. 1907.
Lace in the making, Margaret Brooke, George Routledge & Sons Ltd., 1923.
'Hand-made Bobbin Lace Work' by Margaret Maidment, Pitman & Sons Ltd. 1931.
Art & Illusion, E H Gombrich, Phaidon Press, 1960.
The Chichester Roundel the Otter Memorial Paper no. 4.
West Sussex Institute of Higher Education, 1988
The Winchester Bible, Claire Donovan, Winchester Cathedral , 1993.
New Braids & Designs in Milanese Lace, Patricia Read & Lucy Kincaid, Batsford, 1994.
Ponder These Things, Rowan Williams, Canterbury Press, 2002.
The Macclesfield Psalter Book, The Fitzwilliam Museum, 2005.
Marking the Hours, Eamon Duffy, Yale University Press, 2006.
All about making—Geometrical Bucks Point Lace, Alexandra Stillwell, Salex Publishing, 2006.